The Hoarder
Prose Poems

by

Logan Chace

Finishing Line Press
Georgetown, Kentucky

The Hoarder
Prose Poems

ACKNOWLEDGMENTS

The author would like to acknowledge the following magazines and journals
where these poems originally appeared, sometimes in different versions:

Bear Paw Arts Journal: "Been had been"
Clepsydra Literary and Art Magazine: "As wet as shipwrecks"
Flying Island Literary Journal: "Moths and hummingbirds"
Hive Avenue Literary Journal: "Cathedral light"
LandLocked Magazine: "Places where there weren't even places"
Nobody Thoughts: "I saw him coming" & "House of sighs"

Publisher: Leah Huete de Maines
Editor: Christen Kincaid
Cover Art: Anikha D. Riddick
Author Photo: Corinne Chace
Cover Design: Elizabeth Maines McCleavy

Order online: www.finishinglinepress.com
also available on amazon.com

Author inquiries and mail orders:
Finishing Line Press
PO Box 1626
Georgetown, Kentucky 40324
USA

Contents

To my parents,
whose love for me and for each other never runs dry

Moths and hummingbirds

Little things. The way airborne swarms of dust find their way, like moths, to the stale light of mid-afternoon sun filtering through a window, a wobbly pile of books, a scattering of papers, a lake collecting rain, always remind me of the summer I spent trying to clean out Maggie Harper's house and barn. I was sixteen. The lilacs were still in bloom, but on their way out, swooning over the backyard fence. Life smelled of cut grass, distant grill fires, honeysuckle dizzying the air. Summers still felt almost endless, like the slow roll of a wave, not like the hummingbirds, fluttering, floating, pulsing, then disappearing before you even notice.

Night parachuters

Our college town felt like an island when all the students left for vacation. My parents loved the solitude that it brought, especially my father, a philosophy professor at the school. For me, summers meant sultry idleness, a limbo between the exhilaration of autumn and the chaos of spring. Just before they all moved out for the next three months, I would sit and write what I saw from a picnic table or from my father's office. I had started to write seriously that summer, and these students were my only connection to the real world. Even their unconscious artificiality, their false perceptions of life and of each other seemed genuine to me at the time. I wouldn't be caught dead attending my father's school, no sir, but right then and there, they were all I knew and all I wanted to be.

On move-out days, my friends and I took our backpacks and rode our bikes to the rib-bare campus, the dorms still open for the cleaning crews. We had to time it just right to make sure the cleaners hadn't grabbed all the good stuff yet. Like night parachuters, we slinked through, dorm by dorm, hall by hall, scavenging through closets, ripping through desks and dresser drawers, sweeping under mattresses, ravenous for any loose change, food, clothes, music, magazines, stale cigarettes. The vacant campus seemed to creak and sigh under their absence. Once home, we consumed, amassed, and stashed. We were full, filthy, covetous.

Charity cases

My mother avidly attended church fundraisers. Ham bake sales and clothing drives drove her, kept her going. Between her full-time job as a nurse and her volunteer work at church, helping others in need was her entire existence. I knew that she secretly regretted taking my father's name— Godfrey. Somehow, though, by the grace of God, she never dragged me and my father to church with her, and we never said grace at the dinner table; instead, my mom would grace us with all the charity cases that were being set up for the next couple of weeks. It was during one of these dinner-time sermons that Mom brought up the plan to help Maggie Harper, known hoarder and local loony, clean up her place. I pitied the people who had volunteered for this impossible task, ignorant of what they were getting themselves into. But then, Mom dropped the bomb: "Anyway, I volunteered you, Ben."

Definitely murder

My father looked at me as if he couldn't decide whether to defend and save me or break down laughing at my cruel misfortune. "No way," I blurted out. "Mom, you can't just go around volunteering me for things without asking me. What about the bookstore?"

"You only work at the bookstore two days a week, Ben. You will have time to do other things. It will only be for a week or so. Look, she had a talk with the pastor about cleaning up her place. You know, just airing it out a little bit. Possibly, donating some of it to our drive for the less fortunate. Really, all you need to do is sort through her stuff with her and throw things out."

My dad interrupted, "Didn't I hear something about Maggie Harper a few years back? Something about an accident or killing?"

"A killing," I said. "Like a murder?"

"No, not like a murder," Mom interjected, casting an exasperated glance at my father. "You hear too much gossip down at the diner, Alan." Dad winked at me and whispered, "Definitely murder."

"I don't know, Mom. Sounds kind of dangerous. You really want to send me to the house of a *murderer*?"

"You are not helping, Alan," Mom said. "I already told Pastor Evans that Ben would do it. She just needs someone young and strong to help her haul her trash to the dumpster, or else put her extra clothes and books in bins to bring to church. She might even pay you."

"Wait a minute," I said. "She *might* even pay me? I wouldn't do it for a million bucks."

Where all things go to die

When I climbed the creaking, slanted wooden steps of her front porch, I felt that I would crash right through them, possibly down to the center of the earth. I had always heard that if there was an actual place where the earth ends, where all things went to die, it was Maggie Harper's place; that she hadn't thrown a thing away since 1930. I opened Maggie's warped metal screen door, crusted with dirt and dead insects, ensnared between the rusted squares of the screen, knocked on the front door, the paint of which had been chipped and scratched in streaks as if a gigantic forest creature had slashed it with its claws. "Yes," I confirmed to myself. "I have reached the end of the earth." I almost congratulated myself on my bravery and a life heroically lived, but the door opened sooner than I had prepared myself for. Maybe they were right. Maybe all things did die here. And suddenly, I was a thing.

I saw him coming

towards me, this beanstalk, this tendril-boy, this delicate
watercress: crested with secrets, I guessed, but mostly fettered
with fear. Like I was a snake he knew was hidden somewhere
in the grass. He walked slowly and carefully up the squeaking
steps of my porch, eyes darting all around, waiting for me to
strike, to lurch out with venom in my teeth. I almost had to
laugh. I had asked the church for charity; they brought me
this boy. I knew I would inundate him. I knew I would drive
him away. I knew it wouldn't work, that I couldn't part with
my precious possessions. I peered out at him through my
crusted panes, my once-washed windows when I was a once-
wife, once-mother. This old woman-watcher. This lurker,
onlooking. This lost, lonely, loveless ancient-lady. Desperate,
despondent, dilapidated, drowning. Dunk-drenched.
Discarded by the non-discarded. Scarred. Scared. I opened
the door.

Like caged mice

The first thing I saw was a black hole, and then, the dust clouds trying to escape to the light like caged mice. Then I saw Maggie smiling up at me: frizzy, cloud-gray hair, straw-thin, her face rifted with wrinkles. She took me around the house to her backyard. She walked with a stoop, but at a surprisingly steady pace. Out back, the grass came up to the middle of my calf, and I was already starting to see collected objects spread throughout the field: rusty cans and pails scattered about; old shoes and broken sets of lawn chairs and tables, all partially hidden in the grass. We zigzagged our way through the littered field to a barn, chipped and weathered. Behind the barn, I could see a small lake glittering between the breaks in the trees and tall grass that surrounded it, nearly shrouding it. I thought: I would give anything to scurry to the water and hide forever in the reeds.

Places where there weren't even places

As I walked into the barn, the mix of soured, sodden wood and fabric, the rush and swirl of dirt and dust, and the stale motor oil made me want to forget everything and run home. There was an area of a child's sandbox to enter; the rest of the space was occupied almost floor to ceiling, all around, by heaps of continuous junk: overflowing boxes, random toys, clothes, appliances, pictures, frames, flower pots, rotting furniture, tools, machines; disorganized pyramids of ratty stuffed animals and dolls. Myriads. Some of the dolls were cockeyed, one-eyed, or no-eyed; some had balding hair; some had torn clothes or were naked, their plastic and cotton bodies contorted. Most of all, though, there were stacks of tattered and crumbling books. Some teetered, some had collapsed onto the grubby ground: stuff piled in so many places—places where there weren't even places. The only open space in the barn was the rafters, the lonely beams blanketed in galaxies of cobwebs. There were high wall and ceiling windows, cracked and grimy, and a crooked cupola, where timid sunlight staircased down in weird, serrated angles.

Bookstore stories 1

I had to deal with quite a few Maggies at the small bookstore where I worked downtown. It was next to the bus station, so it brought in some crazies from time to time, people looking for extra cash to get them home. One morning, a ragged looking man came in with sunken sockets, like dredges, barely holding the scooped and cloudy eyes, and asked if I could spare him a few bucks, said he needed to catch the first bus out of town. He went on to tell me that his cheating girlfriend threatened him with a butcher knife, that four years was "enough of that shit." I dug into my pockets and handed him a few folded bills. He crunched the bills in his smudged, shaking fist and thanked me. Small droplets seeped from the holes holding his eyes— streams that stemmed from muddy-bottomed ponds, digging clean grooves into his grainy face.

Bookstore stories 2

Another time, a woman, reeking of days-old clothes and smoke, wrinkled and gaunt-faced, revealing her high-boned cheeks and chin, came in and handed me a torn and stained paperback with its receipt. I told her I couldn't take it back looking like that, and she asked me how, then, could she get home with no money, to a daughter who found it hard to stay away from the drugs and dregs on the street. She couldn't keep the book anyway, see, cause her priest wouldn't allow her to have such filth as romances. I sighed and gave her a few bills. She told me that she had been writing books, too— one on how to stay away from the needle, another on living in a house between two serial killers. She said she would call it *Thirty Years of Terror*.

I took the smoke-stinking book and climbed the ladder. I stood there trying to figure out where to put it among all the blurry titles, how to fit it between the jam-packed paperbacks— self helps; mysteries, comics, plays, and histories; poetry, biographies, and thrillers; the massive collection of bibles— all spine-squeezed and twisted; blood-drained and dead-breathed, the stale and sticking pages that cooked under ticking, blinking fluorescent lights. They were smashed hard into one another, gathering dust on the sagging shelves. This made me think of Maggie—everything she ever got her hands on was packed to the gills in every space she could spare. The objects had massed into one throbbing being, constricted under the heaviness and messiness. I thought our bookstore was overflowing at the time, but it was child's play compared to Maggie.

Cathedral light

We sat on her pool patio with our legs dangling in water, watching the dusk fill up with rainclouds. I had been telling her about Maggie when the rain started falling slowly in large drops. Sarah grabbed my hand: "Let's jump in." The pool water was warm as the air grew cooler around us, and we looked up at the sky, squinting into the rain. It began to downpour, and we spread out on our backs, floating tranquilly in the wavy torrent; we hovered on the undulating water cables, as if the currents of rain that plopped on our faces and the liquid underneath told us that everything we wanted was right there, right then: the sky reflecting a certain rapture. I sank beneath and rested on the pool floor, opened my eyes, and listened to the muted drumming—water on water. We had forgotten to turn the pool light on, so the water was murky gray like an old movie. The bright colors from her house inked through, making it appear as cathedral light—the water's silky underbelly like stone; its surface, the stained glass. I heard the twinkle of wind chimes above. As I saw her push against the wall on the other end of the pool and glide towards me underwater in her baby blue bathing suit, a giant bird fluttered inside my ribcage and soared; I could still feel the branch wobbling from where it took off. And then I was a fish, jerked out of the water by a hook, desperate to catch my breath.

Searching for deer

Sometimes time is a wind tunnel, forcing everything to the side. But other times, time is an open field on an airless evening—slow and thick—bees and butterflies dipping in and out of meadow grass, flowers, and weeds, sparsely-leafed woods to one side, quiet, cautious deer in the distance, and the tips of the orange sun procrastinating on the horizon. That summer was like a field of deer—patient, pensive, not to be bothered. My grandparents used to take me out in the car on these kinds of summer evenings to search for deer in the fields, as if deer were some myth never uncovered, like Sasquatch. On one of these excursions, I heard my grandmother say, "Poor Alan" to her husband. I wanted to know what was so "poor" about my father.

Another time, I came upon my parents talking in quick voices in the upstairs bathroom. I stood outside the door, trying to translate, until my mother realized I was there, came over to me, and asked, "Ben, did you hear anything that your Dad and I were saying?" I shook my head honestly: "No." My childhood was filled with being on the brink of some kind of discovery or comprehension that was well beyond my years, as if true melancholy was something learned. But I could never quite catch sight of the true meaning, like the deer that we barely ever saw on our hunts in the summer sunset fields.

Backdraft

The difference in heat between the stuffy barn and the muggy, rigor-mortised air outside didn't vary so much in degrees, but rather in layers or waves, like stepping out of an oven into a backdraft. The dumpster outside was filling up, but the space in the barn remained the same, as if I was trying to shovel away a Sahara sand dune. After a few more trips, as I lumbered out of the barn with another load, I noticed a figure in the dumpster. Maggie had climbed inside, the top of her shoulders and her head the only visible parts of her body, frantically shuffling around and bobbing down into the refuse to rescue certain valued items like a duck on a pond. "Oh, I can't throw this away," and, "oh no, I need this—this can't go," she muttered, dropping the salvaged materials over the ledge onto the grass below. I don't know how long I stood there with my mouth ajar, watching hours of work disappearing before my eyes, but when I finally made my way to her, she said to me, not even looking up, "I'm sorry dear, but this stuff can't go. There's too much life in it. Here, let me see that." She looked inside my box and took out half of what I had just put in. I leaned my sweaty head against the cool, shaded dumpster, on the brink of giving up. She finally paused from her frenzied rescue mission, her insane dumpster dance, and looked at me, gasping as if woken from a tiring trance, from dreams of strangulation.

Stunned, I stood

there, frozen in the broiling sun, unable to wind myself back up, like my grandmother's grandfather clock that crouched in the corner of my living room, by the couch. How does one get anything done? I smelled the air and thought, someone's smoking something somewhere— probably Rodney reeling in the reeds. How did I let it get this bad? Only my garden grew with any sort of order. I dug the dirt with perfect precision as if it could cancel out the chaos surrounding it. I wished I could bury it all, sink it in soil. But I knew better— Ben and the birds would only find me minutes later, like a dog with its bone, clawing at the clumps, letting the ground leap into the air, filling my lap with it, frantically trying to retrieve everything I had thought I lost.

A garden amidst the wreckage

We both stared at each other, panting, bewildered. Finally, she spoke: "Let's take a break, dear. You must be getting thirsty. And me, I'm just old." Although I wanted to, I hadn't the energy nor the willpower to reject her offer, and I reluctantly followed her back through the maze of trash to her house. Her back porch—as wobbly and warped as the front one—was filled with corroding metal chairs and tables, fence wire, paint cans, and bicycles, all probably unused in decades, like an exhibit from some experimentalist sculptor: rust as the medium. Although, to the left, just before we went into the house, I caught a glimpse of her garden—neatly organized rows of vegetables—beans, tomatoes, beets, cucumbers—then red, yellow, purple, and blue violets, tulips, lilies, and roses.

I thought: what happened to the season of the teenager, those nonexistent, slept-away mornings, those infinite, stifling afternoons that wavered between nothing and sunlight? To the boys of summer? I once misheard that classic rock song as "the poison summer." Was this my poison summer, sickened and spoiled by some old batty's wreckage? Mom was always putting me to work: instead of cleaning out a barn, I had spent the previous summer painting my uncle's. I would wake each morning and place the paint-stained mats, stir the canisters, and set up the ladder; one hand clasped onto the rungs, while the other, the can, veined with dried red drops, and the stiff, paint-caked brush. I now thought of those aging planks, coated with fresh splatter and made a vow: begin again.

Anything you could ever think of

The faded linoleum of the kitchen floor was slanted so that the ratty table and chairs at the other end of the kitchen were at least five inches below the entrance. The ramped floor, the table, counter tops, cabinets, silted windowsills, sink, the top of the refrigerator were all brimming with pots and pans and cans and plants and food and crumbs and screws and nails and magazines and books and utensils and boxes and anything you could ever think of. She had a stack of old calendars and newspapers on the floor and chairs. Coupons were scattered like confetti throughout the kitchen. After a drink, she said, "I think maybe I want too many things, dear. I get lost in it. I know it's overwhelming. I think I try to clutch onto so much because I can't have it all." She folded her arms and embraced herself, retracting into her own shriveling world.

The measurements door

I looked over to my left and spotted a closed door that had ruler markings all the way up, and next to these lines, various dates and increasing ages penciled in. She followed my gaze and said, "Ah, yes. My measurements door. I used to measure Sammy's height every year on that door. Sammy's my boy. He's much older now, though. And much taller, I'm sure. I walked over to the door and studied the map of dates and ages and heights. "Isn't that something," she said. "Look, Ben! You're almost the same height that Sammy was at your age." I saw a line with a "16" and the date "9/15/68" written next to it, but I didn't see any more lines above it. Before I knew it, she had me turned around with my back to the door and a ruler over my head. She reached up and penciled in a wobbly line where she marked my age and the date next to it. "You kids keep growing; I just keep shrinking."

Then, she said, pointing to her measurements door, "But there is no need to go in that room, dear. You can just focus on cleaning the barn and maybe a bit of the rest of the house." But before I could attempt to imagine the horrors on the other side of that door, she quickly added, "I think we've both had enough for one day. See you tomorrow, dear." I burst out into the late afternoon sun. I got onto my bike to head home and looked behind me to watch the dust from the driveway billow up around me and then slowly dissipate into the thickening summer air.

The old sleight of hand

At dinner, I vented to my parents about Maggie, crushed and exhausted. Maggie was crazy, sick, she disgusted me. I wasn't going back there. "Your grandpa was quite the collector, too, you know," my mother said, turning to me. "The old man loved his candy bars, and he would buy bundles of them and hide them from Mom. After a while, he had so many that he would take them out in front of her, and he would have another one waiting when she stole it. He turned into quite the magician, that man."

My grandfather had died the previous Christmas. I easily recalled his constant liveliness, until he couldn't walk anymore, when he began to lose his mind. One night sleeping in my grandparents' room, I woke to my grandpa dreaming. He could barely walk at that point, but he was shouting out in his sleep and bicycling his legs in the air so fast that I swore he was given new life in his underworld of unconsciousness: a carry-over— a quick glimpse of life in this otherworld, those years of life never known to anyone else, and mostly lost to us as well, the dreamers, the authors of that second dimension. I remember Grandma walking him to the bathroom the next morning, saying, "Come on, Lennie. Your legs sure moved faster than that in your sleep last night."

So I could imagine him working the old sleight of hand on my grandma. I pictured him going to the store across the street, an errand for his wife, to pick up a few items, secretly filling his sleeves and pockets with Milky Ways, Fifth Avenues, and Snickers. I saw him sitting down at the kitchen table, casually pulling out the chocolate, peeling the wrapper down midway, and taking his first bite, prepared for his wife's entrance, for her groan, her theft. But as his wife grabbed it out of his hand, he had another out of his sleeve and in his mouth before she even got the first one. The old man's hands were quick; he drew them out of holsters: some in his socks, his shirt pocket, under his hat; some tucked in his belt, another in the back of his collar. I envisioned each one appear and disappear in the place of a new one before his wife could snatch it, her eyes ricocheting all over the room, not able to catch up to one before she spotted another. A point of his finger, a flick of his wrist; a jerk of his neck, his knee against the table; a shift of his eyes and a new candy bar was in and out of his mouth, replaced by the bite of another, as his wife grabbed air. "Give me those damn things," she would squeal and giggle. Eventually, she would give up, sit down and watch the show—this wrinkled illusionist, this charming chocolate bar juggler, winking at her, proud of the few tricks he still had up his sleeve.

"Everyone collects things, Ben," my mom concluded. "Some just don't know how to let go of them." We all had our stories, and we all had our reasons. I decided after dinner to give Maggie another chance.

Honeycomb

Next day, I made a few more trips from the house to the dumpster and then decided to take Maggie's advice and head for the lake. There was a meandering path sprinkled with pine needles that cut through the woods behind the barn. A small, dilapidated dock, lined with tall, green reeds led out into the lake and dunked into the water on one sunken corner. Sunnies circled around their embedded, pebbled nests close to shore. They spawned and danced in spotlight as if choreographed: two to a nest, head to tail, but not in acts of pleasure—more like swimming somnambulists. Across the lake, the nests, dozens of them, connected and spread out like a honeycomb beneath the speckled water. The wind picked up, and a giant white crane sailed out of the trees, glided through the air, and disappeared into the woods on the other side, as if it could both perceive change and search for it at the same time.

As wet as shipwrecks

I could smell the rain again. I looked up, and the sky, unable to make up its mind, clouded over again, beginning to marble-- gray and charcoal. Lightning bolts began to slit the sky; a long roll of thunder spread out across the valley like someone dragging a trash can over a gravelly driveway, and then, like tearing a thick piece of cloth; it ripped a hole right into the fabric of the sky: it opened up and began to downpour, the lake, a bowl, catching the rain in its belly, the water's surface becoming islanded by blots of wind, leaving the ground and trees as wet as shipwrecks. I escaped under a tiny pavilion nearby and thought of Maggie's property—all of her ancient relics, collections, memories, and pain overcrowding the boat, sinking with it, clutter-logged and decaying. And I was the only one leading the expedition to uncover it, trying to restore it without drowning in it myself.

The fisherman

I spotted a man in a large raincoat carrying a bucket and a fishing pole walking my way towards the dock. I couldn't get a good look at his face, hidden under his hood. As he got closer, I could see that he had some small trout strung together on a fishing line. He set the bucket down, leaned his pole against the dock, and spread his fish out like car keys on the slick, wet boards of a picnic table to wash off, then walked under the roof of the pavilion. He lifted off his hood, removed his raincoat, and smiled at me, his teeth, crooked as caves. I could hear his bucket filling up with rain.

The night crawler, the painter

He took a knife out of his pants. "I'm gonna scale these here fish'n get out of the rain, if you don't mind." I watched the knife. I read tomorrow's headline in the lines of his head: *Local Boy Takes the Bait—Escapes Lightning, Can't Escape Fisherman's Knife.* I made up names for him like a game—*The Serial Scaler, The Fugitive Fisherman, Captain Hooks, The Reel Deal, The Cast-Away, The Night Crawler.* He took the fish off the table, knelt down, and began to slice off their scales into the pail. "Believe I'll take these up to my dad's house and filet 'em up real good. I likes 'em with the skin still on 'em is what I like. Make sure all the bones is out and stuff, but I cook 'em with the skin still on. Real tasty." He scraped his knife along the sides of the fish and wiggled them around in the bucket like a painter washing off his brushes.

I watched a bird swoop down, skim the water, then soar to sky. I followed it with my eyes, desperately wanting to mimic its flight away. The fisherman eyed me. "Name's Rodney. You that young kid the church sent to clean out ole Maggie's place? Thought so. I know her pretty good. Time to time I cut her lawn, and she lets me fish here in the lake. Good woman. Has some issues, course. Don't we all. Lost her boy and her man in the same year, one to death, one to divorce. Loved and lost so much, and now she can't let go. I get it, though. So, what's your story, boy?" I don't know why, but I told him I was in love with my best friend, that she had someone else. He nodded as if he knew the whole story. "Been there, brother." When the rain stopped, the fisherman picked a fresh worm out of the drenched dirt and hooked it. I hopped back on my bike and pedaled out into the puddles. I saw him head back toward the river, and then he disappeared behind some trees as if he had never been there at all. I flew away on my bike, my shirt fluttering freely in the breeze.

Mothers and fathers

When I got home Sarah called and wanted to tell me about her new boyfriend, Shane. He was a college kid. All I knew about him was how he had once cupped his hands around his ears at a concert we had attended. I remembered he had looked like a child, trying to ward off the crashing cymbals and the clumsy electric guitars. I could feel something heavy fall out of the branches of my chest and plop noisily into the pond of my stomach.

Sarah had been my best friend since preschool. My parents had been best friends once, too. They had met at bible camp, then inseparable, then only separated by church. My mother still devout, without doubt, my father apathetic, staying in bed on Sunday mornings, snoring, apoplectic, my mother walking downstairs in a flowery dress, shutting the door, sighing, my father waking, reading in blissful silence. I learned from them that faith is like fishing in the fog. I learned that love could be a lake, either flooding out, or shrinking into itself by drought.

That familiar neck

That night I woke to find someone lying next to me in my bed. Shane? My pillow and most of my sheets were stolen by this shadowy being beside me. Sammy? I jumped up, ready to scream, but then I recognized those unkempt eyebrows, that same bare chest and skinny bones. Hands clenched around that familiar neck, I wrestled myself, trying to twist off that mimicking face. I dug my nails into the skin and swung hard uppercuts at the chin and cheek. Then, I gripped the hard knots of shoulders to force my body through the mattress to drown the head—a violent baptism. The torso sunk, but the head remained afloat, mouth wide open, mocking my failed efforts to release me—cut off all ties, like strands of hair. It laughed at me wildly, cursed me, and choked on the heaving mattress waves. It kicked and spat at me, lacing into me. I bit down through tender flesh, grabbed my teeth and ripped off the jawbone, broke off limbs and sinews like those of a fawn, and shattered them over my knee. I spent the rest of the night picking up the strewn parts, trying to mold and meld myself back together again. Exhausted and dripping with hot sweat, I finally woke up in the shivering moonlight.

Ben had been

working all summer, simmering, sweating in the swelter. One step forward, one step back. One afternoon, I slept, woke, wept, remembered how I once wilted into Walter's shoulder, soldered by some slow sonata playing on the stereo, the scratchy record revolving, repeating like past mistakes, especially that one chord that corded us, courted us, quartered us. Later, after Sammy's suicide, Walter waned and wandered, welded and wedded only to himself, wanting to be alone listening to the vinyl's silent confessions, sipping his single malt Macallan on rocks, smoking his Pall Malls in his overalls, always with his albums in his favorite chair, his eyes closed as the light emptied from the sky like a flat tire, darkness deepening like an oil fire, his scotch sucked dry, the room dusted, dazed with a smoke haze, the needle shifting into songless ruts, hiccupping static sighs.

Life moved like this

And just like that, summer vacationed and the students stumbled back in. On move-in day, I rode my bike up to campus and watched them race around with airs of importance, those shrieks of students seeing each other again, carrying bags full of books for their new classes, tossing the Frisbee on the field by the library. There was that buzz you couldn't hear but feel. Before you knew it, they would all be leaving again for the summer like baffled ghosts, shouting about their final grades, as the long train of cars headed off to uncertainty. Life moved like this, I began to learn—that constant spinning vessel. Like the one we rode on at the fairs that made us feel intoxicatingly helpless; it spun so fast it pinned you up to its shiny elliptical walls—recalcitrant, blissfully nauseating, relentless.

Litany for Maggie

Scattered scraps of newspaper clippings, scattered piles of books and magazines making a maze around the house, scattered batteries, lightbulbs, pictures, film cases, scattered crumbs and tableware, utensils, tablecloths, scattered tools— hammers, wrenches, screwdrivers—rusted, broken, scattered video tapes, cassette tapes, CDs, records, scattered lamps, furniture, scattered boxes of clothing, hats, gloves, scarves, purses, suitcases, scattered glass and plastic and cardboard, scattered quilts and sheets and afghans, scattered pens and pencils and paper, scattered board games and cards and dice, scattered dust bunnies, dirt and filth, scattered cans of food, cans of coffee, tins of tea, tins of cookies, scattered slabs of wood and tile and carpet, scattered containers of glue and tape and band aids, scattered cobwebs, scattered clutter in the attic rafters.

Scattered prayers for you, Maggie. Scattered hopes, scattered thoughts, scattered worries, scattered questions, scattered lessons, scattered scolding, scattered praise, scattered promises, scattered curses, scattered hallelujahs, scattered amens.

House of sighs

My mother always called our house the house of sighs, and she usually sighed when she said this. My father let out streams of sighs that filled up the rooms like smoke, at the table, on the couch, on his bed, usually rubbing his head when he did it, as if that was the sighs' secret lair, just beneath his hair. One time, he left his prescription pill bottle out on the counter, and I felt one quark closer to some sort of understanding. My mother sighed when my father sighed, like a giant, empty silo echoing with sighs, and when she went to church. She retreated into her religion, away from him. It never stopped. That summer, I sighed for Sarah— my first crush, my oldest friend, my unrelenting, unrequited love. She never found out. Across town, Maggie must have been sighing under the weight of it all— sighing for Sammy, for her stolen love, for her mountains of possessions. She must have thought there wasn't anyone or anything in the world that thought or cared about her. And suddenly, I was a thing.

A dozen little lives

Sometimes it seems we live a dozen little lives, our timelines divided, our different selves scattered all around, left as remnants. We trudge on with itinerant hearts, itinerant minds. And houses packed to the gills can seem as empty as an expensive, expansive college campus after the students have gone, widened by their leaving, an exhale. We try to clean up, cover up, not repeat the past, but the freshly planted trees and flowers never completely hide the cracks in stone or the tangled ivy on brick—the fault lines and growth of history.

Swallowed whole

by the barn beams, Ben spent his last afternoon on a leaning ladder, sweeping out cobwebs. My mind couldn't help re-entering his room, then reeling, retching, seeing Sammy, my sad son, swinging, sweetly swaying from the ceiling, the frayed strings of rope hanging loose, his noose nested up in the rafters of his room. He was sixteen, just like Ben, though I couldn't bring myself to tell him that. I kept all of Sammy's stuff, buried treasure, in the closet of my measurements door. And there it would stay.

The summer was coming to an end, marked by the last stacked boxes of my memories, still clinging, lingering, not giving in, not admitting defeat. In the late afternoon heat, I gave Ben a gift I had been saving for him, a collection of poems I had recovered from the chaos—*A Boy's Will*—this willful boy, this helpful boy. He hugged me and beamed, this beamish boy, this bird-boy. I was perched on the porch stoop, this rickety house about to collapse about me, but it stayed in place, hanging on by one last nail of hope, hacking and spatting, coughing and sneezing out decades of congestion. After waving goodbye one last time, I went back inside, the house swallowing me whole.

Logan Chace earned an M.F.A. in Creative Writing (Poetry) from Hollins University. He currently teaches English and Creative Writing to high school students at Wyoming Seminary in Kingston, Pennsylvania, where he lives with his wife, Corinne, and his dog, Bennie. Besides writing and teaching poetry, he is a singer/songwriter, who has recorded two albums. His poems and reviews have previously been published in such magazines as *Versal Magazine, The Meadow, Plain Spoke, The Bookends Review, Brushfire, Inlandia, Flying Island, Hive Avenue, Bear Paw Arts Journal,* and *The Hollins Critic.* His debut full-length collection of poems, *After a Night of Drowning,* was published by Kelsay Books in 2022. He has been nominated for a Pushcart Prize.